Stop Anxiety & Panic Attacks

The Ultimate Beginner's Guide to End and Overcome Depression, Social Anxiety and Negative Thinking

By Louise Jiannes

For more great books visit:

HMWPublishing.com

Download another book for Free

I want to thank you for purchasing this book and offer you another book (just as long and valuable as this book), "Health & Fitness Mistakes You Don't Know You're Making", completely free.

Visit the link below to signup and receive it: www.hmwpublishing.com/gift

In this book, I will break down the most common health & fitness mistakes, you are probably committing right now, and I will reveal how you can easily get in the best shape of your life!

In addition to this valuable gift, you will also have an opportunity to get our new books for free, enter giveaways, and receive other valuable emails from me. Again, visit the link to sign up: www.hmwpublishing.com/gift

TABLE OF CONTENTS

Introduction 8

Chapter 1: Let's Get Started 11
    Understanding the Anxiety Problem 11
    How is Anxiety a Normal Reaction? 11
    How is Anxiety a Problem? 13
        Overview of Anxiety Disorders and Its Symptoms 15
        Generalized Anxiety Disorder (GAD) 15
        Panic Disorder (PD) 16
        Social Anxiety Disorder (SAD) 19
        Obsessive–Compulsive Disorder (OCD) 21
    Understanding The Causes of Anxiety Disorders 23
        Prenatal Environment 23
        Early Childhood Experience 25
            Temperament 28
            Modeling 31
            Attachment 33
            Trauma 34
        Medical and Substance-Related Considerations 35
        Is Being Anxious All Bad? 37

Chapter 2: Are You Sure It Is Anxiety? 40
    Seeing The Doctor 40
    What Will the Doctor Do? 42

How Shall I Talk to The Doctor? 42
What Will Happen Next? 44
    Wait and See 44
    Tranquilizers 44
    Other Medication 44
    Counseling 45
    Referral to A Mental Health Unit 45

Chapter 3: Dealing with Physical Symptoms 46
    Controlled Breathing 47
    Progressive Muscle Relaxation 50
    Curtail Caffeine Consumption 53

Chapter 4: Practical Ways to Help Overcome Anxiety 56
    Take a Pause 56
    Acceptance 58
    Declutter 60
    Do Some Positive Self-Talk 62
    Getting Involved in Physical Activities 66
    Examining Your Diet 68
        Foods that Alleviate Anxiety 68
        Eat Foods with Nutrients 69
        Essential Antioxidants on your Plate 69
        Eat the "Right Carbs" to Calm your Mind 70
        Foods That May Help with Anxiety 71

Nuts 71
Fresh fruit and vegetables 71
Chamomile and green tea 72
Wholegrain bread 73
Cottage cheese 73
Oatmeal 73
Brain Food 73
Getting Enough Sleep 73
Relax your Breathing 75
Meditation 77
Relax your Muscles 79
Practicing Mindfulness 82
Turn Fears into Inspirations 84

Chapter 5: Action Plan I – Dealing with Anxious Thoughts.. 87

How to Start? 93
   Prepare a Thought Record 93
   Determine the Realistic Thoughts from Anxious Thoughts 93
   Assessment 95

Chapter 6: Action Plan II – Dealing with Worries 96

Understanding Worrying 96
How Can You Manage Worrying? 99

Chapter 7: Action Plan III – Dealing with Avoidance 102

   Three Things You Can Do Towards Managing Avoidance 104

Final Words 106

Conclusion 109

About the Co-Author 110

Introduction

This book, *A Self-Help Approach to Overcome Anxiety: Eliminating Negative Thinking, Insecurities, Worries, and Depression* contains proven steps and strategies on how to manage anxiety.

No matter how strong, well-bred, or exemplary you have been in life, you cannot deny the fact that at some point or the other you must have felt anxious. There is not a single human being alive who hasn't undergone or experienced anxiousness in his or her life. This assertion is enough to state that anxiety is perfectly normal, and people who suffer from anxiety are ordinary and normal people.

This brings us to the most important question that the book is expected to answer: what is anxiety? Anxiety is an emotion that the human body produces when it is faced with situations of threat or when the individual feels that he or she will not be able to cope with the situation on his or her own. If you attempt to list out the situations or circumstances that have made you anxious, I am sure you will list something like "first job interview" or a "public speech," to name a few.

The situations and circumstances that will make you anxious cannot be predicted with any percentage of probability given the fact that the situations that you perceive as threatening may not be threatening to me, so my body does not react the same way your body does. The intensity of this perception also varies from individual to individual, and so does the reaction. It is precisely as simple as this.

That being said, some people feel anxious at things that are otherwise not considered threatening much more than others, and the reaction generated by them is also rather grave. This reaction can be unbearable for some people so much so that it starts interfering with their day-to-day life, hindering the way in which they lead their lives. Coping with such situations and people suffering from situations can be rather difficult.

If you are someone facing the anxiety issue or are associated with someone who is, this book is a perfect guide to help you understand the problem. Moreover, it shall also help you learn techniques and ways to deal with such situations immediately on the long-term basis.

Before you begin, start with an open mind, and by no means consider yourself or the individual facing the anxiety issue "abnormal." The situation is challenging, but it is manageable. Read the book to know why and how. I hope you enjoy it!

Chapter 1: Let's Get Started

Understanding the Anxiety Problem

Although the anxiety problem is unpleasant and excessively disturbing both to the individual concerned and the people around him or her, anxiety is absolutely normal and harmless. Some of the initial symptoms that a person may experience due to anxiety include increased heart rate, nervousness, and shortness of breath, in addition to several others. In fact, the list of symptoms that are classified as an anxiety response is quite extensive. This response is usually triggered by a situation that is seemingly threatening for the individual.

How is Anxiety a Normal Reaction?

Whenever an individual is faced with a situation that his or her body considers threatening and potentially harmful, the body responds with physical and mental reactions to help the individual deal with the situation. Therefore, the symptoms of anxiety are actually present with the intention to help the individual in the time of crisis. This makes anxiety a helpful bodily response.

For instance, if you are standing on top of the cliff, you are likely to experience an anxiety reaction. Your heart rate may increase, your hands feel clammy, or maybe your muscles will tense up. The intent behind this reaction is to motivate you to move back and save you from the potential harm of falling off the cliff. Technically, such a bodily response is called the "fight or flight" response. This bodily response is a response that is conditioned and developed by the human body as a result of the experiences we have had in our lives. The increased heart rate increases the blood flow in the body's muscles, and high breathing improves the flow of oxygen in the body. Most of the other symptoms are meant towards preparing the body for the danger to come. Once the danger is over, the body returns to normalcy.

How is Anxiety a Problem?

If anxiety is such a normal response of the human body, what makes it such a huge problem? Why is it that some people feel extremely anxious in some situations while others consider it normal and non-threatening? The background and past experiences of the individual are largely responsible for how he or she reacts to a situation.

The four fundamentals of anxiety are thought, emotion, response, and avoidance behavior. Elaborating on these four fundamentals of anxiety and its response, the individual's thoughts are full of negativity, foreseeing anger and potential threat. Moreover, the individual also begins to believe that he or she will not be able to cope with these thoughts, as they seem too overpowering. These thoughts give rise to emotions of nervousness, which reflects in physical symptoms like trembling. The experience alters the behavior of the individual forever. The individual will start fearing such situations and will attempt to avoid them, adding to the fear all the more.

Now that you have an idea about the problem and what anxiety is capable of doing to you, the rest of the book focuses on helping you deal with the anxiety on both the psychological and physiological levels. As you go through the rest of this book, try to apply the advice provided here to your own situation to achieve the greatest outcome: anxiety relief.

Overview of Anxiety Disorders and Its Symptoms

Generalized Anxiety Disorder (GAD)

If you have GAD, worrying may be your main pastime. Everyday occurrences give you more cause for concern than they do for those around you. A barrage of "what ifs" can ruin a simple activity like going to the grocery store, having a health check-up, or sending your daughter off on her first day of school. "What if the car gets a flat? What if the doctor finds something wrong? What if my daughter doesn't like her new teacher, forgets her lunch, falls and scrapes her knee at recess and then the kids laugh at her and then her knee gets infected?" The list can go on and on. Along with this chronic worry can come the chronic physical discomfort of stomach aches or other gastrointestinal upsets, tension headaches, and the fatigue that comes from constantly being on edge.

If you have GAD, therapy or self-help techniques can help you regain the sense of emotional well-being that comes with relinquishing your constant worries and the physical well-being that happens when your body is no longer operating in a state of chronic stress. Life needn't be merely a progression from one worry to the next. Therapy can help reintroduce you to the richness and fullness of a life free of chronic anxiety.

Panic Disorder (PD)

If you have PD, you have had at least one panic attack. Like my attack described above, this consists of an episode in which you experience intense fear accompanied by physical sensations such as a racing heartbeat, shortness of breath, and hot or cold sweats, just to name a few. People who experience such attacks often fear they are having a heart attack or other medical emergency. You also might fear you are losing your grip on reality and think you are going "crazy."

If you have PD, however, you probably frequently worry about when and where you might have another panic attack. You play possible scenarios of your next attack in your mind and begin to avoid the places where you fear another attack is likely to occur. Some people become so fearful of having a panic attack in a public place that they rarely venture from their house.

This anticipatory worry about panic attacks and avoidance is what distinguishes people with PD from those who, like me, have an occasional panic attack. With treatment, the fear of having a panic attack will no longer rule your life. You can learn that, as counterintuitive as it may seem, even a panic attack provides no reason to panic. As panic loses its power, you can regain the sense of agency and competency that you lost to your fear of panic and more.

Specific Phobias (SP)

Phobias are an extreme fear of a particular thing or situation. Common specific phobias include fear of roaches, spiders, snakes, needles, heights, etc. If you have a phobia, you recognize that your fear is irrational. There's no logical reason you can think of for the sight of your phobic object or situation to inspire such extreme terror. But reason with yourself as you might, your extreme fear does not decrease.

Like people with panic disorder, you are likely to avoid that which you fear. But unlike people with PD, you probably don't spend much time worrying about encountering your phobic object or situation. Thus, phobias generally do not affect people's lives as pervasively as do the other anxiety disorders covered in this book. For that reason, people are less likely to enter into therapy for the treatment of a phobia. If you do have a phobia, however, treatment is well worth your while. There are many simple and effective treatments for phobias. Rather than attempting to steer clear of your phobia for the rest of your life, it is recommended to give the treatment a try.

Social Anxiety Disorder (SAD)

If you have a social anxiety disorder, you most likely have an intense fear of being seen, criticized, or judged by others. This probably leads you to limit your social activities and curtail your professional or academic life. You might be afraid to go to parties, participate in class, or attend staff meetings; public speaking might be unbearable to you. You might feel dread for days or weeks in anticipation of the situations or events you fear or avoid them entirely.

Likewise, your choice of job and decision to pursue or forego higher education might be dictated by your fears and avoidances due to social anxiety. In some cases, people with severe SAD are afraid of answering the phone, eating or writing in front of others, or using public toilets. Physical symptoms associated with this disorder include heart palpitations, faintness, blushing, and profuse sweating when confronted with the social situations that you fear, giving you yet another reason to avoid them.

With treatment, social situations will no longer trigger this hotbed of physical discomfort and emotional unrest.

Obsessive–Compulsive Disorder (OCD)

Recently there have been many portrayals of characters with obsessive-compulsive disorder in movies and television shows. They show people who are so afraid of being contaminated by germs that they wash their hands compulsively, wear gloves in public, and always have hand sanitizer nearby. Or you might have seen a character who needs to flip each light switch on and off three times when entering or to exit a room or perform other repetitive checking and counting rituals throughout the day. All of these behaviors fit some of the many symptoms of OCD.

If you have OCD, you experience persistent, recurring thoughts (obsessions) that center around a given theme, such as fear of germ contamination. To quell these fears, you usually develop a ritual or routine (compulsion) that calms the anxiety spurred by the recurring obsession. Other compulsive rituals can include repeating phrases or tasks, hoarding items, and needing physical objects in your surroundings to be perfectly symmetrical or aligned. Regardless of the particular obsession or response behavior, if you have OCD, you feel as if you must engage in your particular ritual (or in some cases, an avoidance) whenever your obsessive thoughts occur. Treatment can help you to move beyond your obsessions to a way of life in which your obsessions and compulsions don't hold you, hostage, any longer.

You can see that common to all of the anxiety disorders is a pervasive sense of fear and uneasiness that interferes with your ability to feel that you are okay and that takes a toll on your body as well as your mind. People with anxiety disorders are more likely to experience heightened levels of anxiety-related physical discomfort and to notice these sensations more acutely than someone without an anxiety disorder. They are also more likely to misinterpret and overreact to these symptoms, often creating a vicious cycle. In response, people often seek help from physicians to fix physical symptoms that are brought about by an anxiety disorder. In fact, in 1999, a study commissioned by the Anxiety Disorder Association of America found that Americans spent more than $22.84 billion in repeated visits to healthcare facilities due to physical symptoms of anxiety disorders.

Luckily, there is a solution. With effective therapy, relief from this self-perpetuating cycle is within reach.

Understanding The Causes of Anxiety Disorders
Prenatal Environment

Right from the womb, we can be affected by our mother's stress. The mother and developing fetus share the same blood, and stress hormones produced by the mother cross the placental blood barrier. Thus a pregnant mother's stress can have a cascading effect: stress the mother experiences can be transmitted into the body of the developing child via an increase in stress hormones. Of course, pregnant women, just like anyone else, experience the ups and downs of life, and the resulting stress is reflected physiologically. Moderate levels of stress are typical and have not been shown to harm a baby's in-utero development. However, heightened stress over an extended period will cause the mother's system to maintain an excessive amount of stress hormones, which flood the baby's newly developing nervous system, propelling the baby into a state of chronic stress.

According to some researchers, mothers who experience a significant amount of anxiety during pregnancy have been shown to have infants who display many markers of an overly charged nervous system. From temperament to motor development, in-utero stress levels appear to make a difference. Highly anxious pregnancies tend to produce anxious babies. Thus, a pregnant mother's emotions and the resulting in-utero environment correlate with an infant's physiological and emotional reactivity.

Early Childhood Experience

The infant brain can be thought of as a vast network of possibilities. By the time a child reaches eight months of age, she is estimated to possess one thousand trillion synaptic connections – twice that of the average adult. If the brain were an information highway, neurons would be the pavement that makes up the roads. Neurons connect to one another at junctions called synapses, like the tracks of a large train set, too intricate to thoroughly map, with pathways exponentially more interconnected than the roads on any city map. It is from this overabundance of possible channels that roads are either reinforced and strengthened by use or discarded by lack of use.

The experiences during an individual's life determine which pathways are reinforced and which are discarded. This process, known as pruning, occurs primarily during the first twelve years of life, but the 1-3 years of life are the most critical period of pruning. For instance, as a baby practices grasping a rubber ball, neural connections that facilitate grasping are reinforced. In the same way, if a baby cries and consistently receives comfort in response, neural pathways will be paved. If a baby's cries bring harsh treatment or bring no one at all, the brain will pave a different road entirely. Hence, an adult has only half the synapses of an eight-month-old child, and they were sturdily and selectively paved.

The pruning process is profoundly influenced by the relationship between the infant and her parents. The baby's information about the world comes mainly from those who are holding, feeding, changing, and otherwise caring for the child. Thus infant-caregiver relationships strongly impact the first paving of the network of neuronal roadways. The infant is dependent on relationships to have her most basic needs met. Hence when there is some rift in relational support, it can have far-reaching effects on the laying and trafficking of neuronal roadwork. Unfortunately, babies who experience a lot of stress or trauma adapt in such a way that they maintain or produce excessive levels of stress hormones even in routine situations that other babies would not find threatening.

Again, experience colors genetic expression. But what of characteristics that appear more innate, more consistent over time and resistant to the coloring of experience? Temperament is such a construct.

Temperament

Children are born with different temperaments. Many parents, often reporting marked differences in the personalities of their children, corroborate the idea of innate temperament.

Research from the field of developmental psychology supports these informal observations of parents. Temperament is a component of personality style, and as such remains stable over time. Aaron Beck, a psychiatrist well known for his treatment of anxiety and depression, found that differences in temperament contribute to different reactions to stress and ways of coping with stress. Jeffrey Young, psychologist and author of Schema Therapy, identified such innate temperamental traits in infants as anxious v. calm and irritable v. stable.

Jerome Kagan, a researcher in developmental psychology, found that 15% to 20% of American and European children were born with a "behaviorally inhibited temperamental style" In other words, certain infants with the inhibited style were unusually anxious in new situations and displayed physiological responses such as rapid heartbeat and higher levels of stress hormones. He also found that inhibited baby boys became shy toddlers, while inhibited baby girls became restless little girls. It is not a far leap to hypothesize that a toddler who displays increased heartbeat and cortisol levels in novel situations might be prone to developing an anxiety disorder in adulthood. However, it is important to note that an anxious temperament early in life sets nothing in stone about later life.

Although adults with anxiety disorders often displayed inhibited responses as children, not all children with anxious temperaments become anxious adults. This fact suggests that other variables affect the outcome. We have seen how in-utero environment and infant-caregiver relationships can color the polygenic expression of anxiety. We know that soothing, nurturing family environments can mitigate innate personality styles. In childhood, modeling and learned attachment styles are critical to the laying of neuronal roadways and the maps that result. This can work to the child's benefit when a child with an anxious temperament learns adaptive means of coping from caregivers. Unfortunately, the importance of modeling can work to the child's detriment when caregivers model less adaptive, more anxiety-fueling behaviors.

Modeling

Parents' consistent emotional nurturance predicates optimum, healthy cognitive and emotional development on the part of the child. Parenting styles that create emotional malnourishment have consequences for a child's emotional and cognitive growth.

It is not surprising that a child's perception of his parents' attitudes and expressions of anxiety influences and nourishes his emotional development. Our actions, words, body language, the risks we take, the risks we avoid, communicate to our children whether the world is a place where we can thrive, or where we should remain on edge, fearful and reticent at every turn.

Overprotective parents inadvertently injure their children via the implication that the world is unsafe and that the children lack the resources to handle challenges. They often explain in great detail the dire consequences that can occur in their children when they venture into the world.

Anxious parenting also harms children by engendering a lack of self-agency, the sense that they, not someone else, are the agents that produce the desired outcome. In other words, an A student whose parents excessively edit his school papers likely would not gain a sense of self-agency regarding his school work and ultimately would doubt his own ability to succeed academically.

Similarly, overprotective parents impede the development of self-efficacy, the sense that one can take effective actions. Individuals with diminished self-efficacy are less resilient to stress and underestimate their resources.

Attachment

When there is a lack of support and emotional attunement in infant-parent and childhood relationships, less-than-optimal attachment styles arise. Trauma experts noted that some anxious mothers had a diminished capacity to respond sensitively to the needs of their children, either under or overreacting to their children's needs. The result was that when the children became distressed, rather than seek their parents for comfort, they distanced themselves from their parents. This makes sense, given that the children did not experience their mothers as being responsive to their needs. Not only did they develop a pattern of seeking isolation rather than interaction, but they also didn't receive the nurturance needed to eventually learn self-soothing techniques, a skill essential to managing their own emotions throughout their lives.

Trauma

It is widely recognized that childhood trauma resulting from abuse, neglect, or illness or injuries requiring invasive medical interventions affects the development of the brain and thereby shapes future behaviors and reactions.

Allan Schore, the neuroscience writer and psychiatry researcher, wrote, "the dysregulating events of both abuse and neglect create chaotic biochemical alterations in the infant's brain." Trauma also significantly alters the neurochemicals that travel along the networks, which can increase the risk of developing anxiety and of diminished resilience to stress. The message encoded in the brain as the result of childhood trauma is that the world is unsafe. Danger lurks. These damaging effects of trauma can result from prolonged or acute events and even from events later in life.

Medical and Substance-Related Considerations

In exploring what's behind symptoms of anxiety, it's important to remember the intricate connection between the physical body and emotions. Not all individuals who have physical symptoms of panic or anxiety have an anxiety disorder. Some medical conditions are real and treatable causes of the physiological and psychological distress associated with anxiety disorders. Shortness of breath that snowballs into hyperventilation may arise from undiagnosed or improperly treated asthma. Palpitations of the heart related to panic may be caused by hyperthyroidism or cardiac arrhythmias or certain medications. Tremors and cold sweats can be symptoms of hypoglycemia. Hormone imbalances, including those some women experience during menopause, can dramatically affect the intensity of anxiety.

What we take into our bodies can also be the source of heightened anxiety. Psychoactive street drugs, such as speed or cocaine, are often the first example that comes to mind. Less obvious are the secondary side effects of some prescription medications, such as the steroids in some asthma inhalers, or the overuse of over-the-counter medications, such as a headache or non-drowsy cold medications containing acetaminophen and caffeine. It is easy to underestimate the effects of seemingly mild stimulants such as caffeine or nicotine that can build up gradually on a day-to-day basis. Mild, undiagnosed food allergies can also be the source of anxiety. When considering the causes of anxiety, it is erroneous to jump to psychophysiological explanations before ruling out medical or substance-related causes. A trip to the physician can be just as crucial as a trip to the psychotherapist.

Is Being Anxious All Bad?

It's natural, but not helpful, to focus only on the negatives of anxiety. Sure, you suffer more than you need to, and you miss some of today's pleasures because you are worrying about tomorrow. However, being anxious is not all bad. Because of your anxiety, you are careful, alert, and cautious. You rarely make careless mistakes. You are prepared for every eventuality.

I know some people who are anxious. They are generally careful about what they put in their bodies, and they read the inserts about the side effects of their prescriptions. They think carefully about risks and decisions. They look ahead for the potholes on the streets and manage to avoid everyone. They anticipate what can go wrong in their lives and try their best to circumvent these possibilities.

Of course, you don't want to suffer intense anxiety, and you don't have to. But you can allow yourself to enjoy and appreciate the positive side of anxiety while you have it. Caution, carefulness, and even vigilance are valuable qualities,

On the flip side, it is an absolute fact that no matter how anxiety disorders affect you, they create suffering. Anxiety disorders rob you of the pleasure of the now as you focus intently on the fears of the future. It's like borrowing trouble, suffering in advance. Your anxiety can overburden your relationships, restrict your activities, deplete your self-confidence, and compromise the ease with which you navigate your life. But despite all these challenges, like most people who are plagued with anxiety, you are stronger than you think.

Missionary Sister Busche noted, "We are like tea bags—we don't know our strength until we're in hot water." As you face the challenges of overcoming an anxiety disorder, I hope you will delight in the discovery of the inner resources within yourself that you are just beginning to tap.

Chapter 2: Are You Sure It Is Anxiety?

Those who experience their first panic attack might think they have a heart attack. As a result, someone might call for an emergency ambulance. Once admitted, some tests will be conducted to them and only to tell that it is panic. A typical reaction would be embarrassment and doubt, but what matters is that they have been checked by a doctor and understand the occurrences that happened to them. However, on the other side of the gauge, some are suffering from this illness for years without professionally diagnosed, without telling anyone about it and not receiving any help.

Seeing The Doctor

Everyone needs to be checked by a doctor to whom they can discuss their symptoms and get a proper diagnosis. There are some physical illnesses which symptoms are alike with anxiety, so they need to clarify if you are suffering from any of those illnesses. Now, if you have a thyroid problem, there is no need for you to further check this book as this kind of illness can be treated with medication.

Have you ever seen your doctor? If not, then, it is time to have yourself checked. If you are worried about doing this, opt for having someone to accompany you for support. What you should keep in your mind is, if the result of the diagnosis is an Anxiety disorder, know that it is an illness and not your fault. You should not be embarrassed about it.

Some might worry about their medical records stating they have an anxiety problem and this might affect them in many ways. However, this problem is quite common, but those people with a similar problem as yours are now enjoying a happy and fulfilling life. Would you not wish to be one of them?

What Will the Doctor Do?

Expect that a doctor will pay attention to the things you will say and ask you relevant questions. To rule out a physical cause, a doctor will do some simple check. For example, if showing a needle to be used for a blood test caused you uncomfortable, tell it.

How Shall I Talk to The Doctor?

Some people might worry about how they are going to explain their anxiety. To help you express your feelings, you may want to have a list of the sensations you had. When talking about a specific incident, you don't need to elaborate much on it. A simple statement will do, and the doctor will just ask questions to acquire more info.

Examples:

"I was waiting behind the stage before presenting when I suddenly felt sick. My heart beats too fast, and my legs were shaky."

"I feel so stuck in the morning that I just can't get out of my bed. I get worse as the day goes on."

"I don't know, but I need to check that the door is locked. I know I locked it, but sometimes I go back more than ten times to it. It takes a lot of my time in the morning to stop myself from doing it."

These are just some of the few statements to get started. At first, it will be hard for you to ask questions that confuse you: "Am I crazy?" "Can I stop my heart from pounding too fast?" It's okay. You have made a start.

What Will Happen Next?

Here are some of the possible suggestions of the doctor to help you.

Wait and See

If your anxiety is new, it a practical idea to wait for weeks to check if it will subside. Your doctor will give you a timeframe and note certain changes.

Tranquilizers

Even if tranquilizers are known to be addictive when used for long-term, taking it on a short course can help overcome a hard phase.

Other Medication

Your doctor might suggest you try beta-blockers or antidepressants. To know which of these is the right one for you, you may need to try more than one anti-depressant.

Counseling

A counselor talks to the patients. You need to set an appointment if it is suggested to you.

Referral to A Mental Health Unit

If you are asked to undergo therapy, the most common approach you will be using is the Cognitive Behavior Therapy. It is known to be the most successful therapy for treating Anxiety. This book is also based on this technique, and you will know more about it as you go through the pages.

Chapter 3: Dealing with Physical Symptoms

Before we move on to management techniques, let us discuss the ways and means by which anxiety can affect you physically.

One of the most noticeable physical effects of anxiety is the respiratory response. When an individual is experiencing anxiety, his or her breathing begins to increase. This reaction is part of the fight or flight bodily response; an individual's breathing will become shallow and incomplete. The objective here is to prepare the body for exertion. Exertion is associated with an increased need for oxygen in the blood vessels and muscles. The body furnishes this increased demand for oxygen in the brain by triggering the breathing process to acquire more oxygen in little time.

To manage the physical symptoms associated with anxiety, we will discuss you the techniques that might be most effective for your case.

Controlled Breathing

As previously mentioned, the most common physical symptom of anxiety is the quick and shallow breathing response. The more an individual tries to get a hold of his or her breathing by gasping for air, the more his or her problem worsens, and the whole process can lead to immense discomfort. The physical response is called over-breathing.

To negate the effects of this response, you need to follow what is called controlled breathing. This type of breathing can play an instrumental role in helping you address several physical issues associated with anxiety.

When anxiety strikes, you must make a conscious effort to take a deep breath in, and then breathe out carefully and attentively. Inhale to your full capacity. That is, breathe in until your lungs feel full, and then exhale slowly. Try to control your breathing pattern in such a manner that your breathing is slowed down yet is evenly distributed.

To practice controlled breathing, you need to mark out a time in your schedule for the same. Choose a time when you are least likely to be disturbed by anyone. Find a quiet place for yourself so you can sit with all your attention and focus. Try not let anything distract or disturb you. Once you are ready to go, follow these steps:

1. Focus on how you are breathing right now. Let yourself relax. Pay attention to whether you are breathing fast or slow; is there a rhythm to your

breathing? Or is it irritate? Now, place one of your hands on your chest and place the other hand on your stomach. Take a deep breath and try to fill your stomach with air, followed by your lungs. You should notice your hand on your stomach rise, followed by the hand on your chest. If you notice ample movement on both your hands, you can assume that you are breathing fully. However, please note here that your chest will not swell as much as the stomach.

2. Once you inhaled fully, it is time to exhale. Let the exhaling action be just as slow and gentle as the inhaling process. As you exhale, imagine all your worries, anxieties, and anticipations flowing out your body. You will feel a sense of cleansing at this time. Perform the inhale-exhale process a couple of times to get used to the rhythm.

3. After you have pickled your breathing rhythm, do it attentively. If you are too anxious, you will realize that your mind will wander a lot throughout this activity so you must bring your focus back every single time to the breathing pattern. Spend time practicing this activity on a daily basis or as needed.

Progressive Muscle Relaxation

Another physical symptom that results from anxiety is stretched muscles, such as a stiff neck and tight chest. This type of tension is evidence that the body is under immense stress. To avoid the effects of the muscle tension and stress, you must learn to relax your body at such times. One of the most important aspects of relaxation is to identify when your body has started getting tense. Once you learn to identify this, performing the relaxation exercise is just a matter of practice.

To practice progressive muscle relaxation, follow these simple steps."

1. Find a quiet and relaxing place that you can sit or lie down comfortably, and where you will be undisturbed for some time. Be sure to wear clothes that fit comfortably and do not add any element of stress to your body.

2. Take a few deep breaths and allow your body to loosen up. This is the perfect time to utilize the controlled breathing exercise that I just mentioned. As you are breathing, do not forget to focus on your breathing pattern and muscle relaxation shall follow.

3. Alternatively, stretch and relax your muscles. Tighten your muscles for 5 seconds and feel the stretch as it rolls through our body. Once the allowed time is over, let the muscles relax for the

next 5 seconds. Perform this activity with special attention to the limbs. Notice the sensation in your body while it is transitioning from a state of the tension to a state of relaxation. Once you can feel the relaxed sensation in our limbs, you can switch to other muscle groups such as the back, stomach, thighs, and calves.

4. You should repeat each stretch 5 to 7 times for maximum effectiveness. Lastly, you can assume that your body is back into a relaxed mode if your breathing has regularized and deepened.

With time, you will realize that relaxation requires a good amount of practice. Typically, you should practice more relaxation exercises two times a day for 30 minutes sessions each. However, you can form a schedule that best suits your needs and gives you the best level of relaxation.

Another important thing to note here is that you must not shock your body. Once you have gone through the muscle relaxation exercise, and your body is totally relaxed, do not stand up right away. Let your body adjust to the newfound environment and get up gently and slowly.

If you have been having a hard time with anxiety lately, it is a good idea to maintain a diary in which you note down all the times you feel most anxious, the reasons for the anxiety, and how well the relaxation exercise helped you to overcome your anxiety. Make notes on the things that have improved due to the relaxation exercise for you and attempt to understand why. The objective of keeping a log is to assess your progress as you practice relaxation.

Curtail Caffeine Consumption

The beverages we drink have an important and significant impact on our mental status. The reason behind this impact is a compound called caffeine, which is a stimulant. If you are anxious, the last thing on your list must be caffeine. You just cannot afford to have it. In fact, many people have realized that reducing their caffeine intake has reduced their anxiety levels substantially. This has even been the case of people who have consumed moderate amounts of caffeine in their daily diet.

If you are unsure as to what contains caffeine, it is always a good idea to check the ingredients listed on the labels. Tea, coffee, chocolate, and most carbonated drinks contain caffeine. Try to restrict your consumption by monitoring the number of caffeinated drinks you consume on a daily basis. If keeping track of such things sounds like a struggle to you, you should really consider maintaining a diary for that purpose.

As you attempt to reduce your caffeine consumption, be aware that caffeine is an addictive compound. If you are used to consuming it in large quantities, you may have to deal with withdrawal symptoms like fatigue and headaches. Therefore, reduce your consumption on a gradual basis by tapering off your intake. Putting a sudden stop on your consumption will not be of great help to your situation.

Chapter 4: Practical Ways to Help Overcome Anxiety

Take a Pause

If you truly understand the dynamic of anxiety, then you can easily translate it using a few words. Those words will be: "Pause because you are hurt."

Anxiety is actually a reminder that perhaps, stimuli around you are hurting too much already to the point that you already need to take a short pause. The most logical step is to stop for a bit and not to stay at that state – staying right there will render you paralyzed. What you need to do is to find where you are hurting to address it appropriately. The level of severity of the hurt is actually directly related to the scope of damage.

The method and strategy of taking a pause can come in many variations. The following are some of the known ways: having a racing heart, taking a deep and heavy breath, constantly obtaining the feeling of dissociation, and spinning your thoughts. Feel free to choose whichever you feel be the most effective. Personalization and customization of ways is something that you should do to address anxiety effectively.

Taking a pause is okay because it helps you avoid getting to the peak of anxiety. It is better to stop to address the fears right away rather than suppress it deep within. Suppressing the fear might lead to a much more difficult situation that you can't handle anymore.

Here's the thing, if your problem is truly anxiety, then you have nothing to fear because anxiety itself won't hurt you. It is the actions you take after that might hurt you. So, regularly take that pause to check where you are really hurting.

Acceptance

Anxiety is something that you need to befriend and make friends with as soon as possible. From time to time, you need to speak to yourself and reflect on your anxiety. You need to constantly reassure yourself and tell yourself that you are truly okay. Listen to your heart and your mind. Pay attention to what your heart is craving for. Pay attention to the issues that matter to you. Find the peace within.

Befriend and making peace with your anxiety will help you find some proactive ways to address it. On the other hand, suppressing it will only be good as denying it.

By denying its existence, you are allowing it to persist and to grow continuously and exponentially.

The true key to obtaining a real solution for the anxiety problem actually lies with acceptance. If you take longer to persist within your comfort zone, blame other people and external factors for the circumstances that you are facing, the longer it will take you to find the hidden opportunities and solutions to your problem connected to anxiety.

For some spiritual experts, acceptance is one step towards feeling better and being better.

Once you accept what you fear, there is a chance that you would cease fearing it. At the very least, the intensity of your fear might be lessened.

As you take the long journey towards accepting something, you will begin to feel a bit better about your life and yourself. If you begin to realize that you have several options available at hand, then you can freely go out of your comfort zone. If you want to outgrow your fear and anxiety, you need to embrace and accept your present circumstances. Also, you can find there's more to life.

Declutter

Physical clutter is a manifestation of a deeper problem. It can be a sign of fear and anxiety piling up in your heart and your mind. For example, if your workplace is a mess, then you might find it difficult to take some short breaks. It will also make you feel like the work that you have seems not end. It will somewhat feed your fears within because you are swimming into your stress. So, you need to take fifteen short minutes every day to tidy up a bit your home or your work area.

A clean workplace and a clean home is not only an organized space; it is also a space that tends to drive away stress, fear, and anxiety. It will help you think more logically. Rationality usually takes over an organized workspace.

Again, if clutter at home or the workplace can mean something more serious, then what should be done? To avoid the ill effects of excessive clutter, you will need to keep an eye on your day to day affairs. For examples, you need to keep everything within the manageable level.

According to experts, the clutter around you somewhat weighs you down because you will feel less confident about yourself. Disorderliness leads to having fewer accomplishments, and it leads to a lower level of self-esteem. When you are not accomplishing enough, you tend to question your capability, and you also tend to dread what coming in the future.

To move forward, inevitably, you need to reduce the clutter to cut down the level of stress that can be caused by it. If you can do this properly, you will get the most amazing rewards, namely: a very attractive place of abode, a significantly lowered level of stress and a more organized and highly productive kind of life.

But of course, you need to begin with the most basic things: you have to declutter your house, your place of work, and of course, your life.

Do Some Positive Self-Talk

Thinking positively will help you manage stress and fight off fears and anxiety. However, if you are the type who tends to practice negative self-talk, you must make it a point to unlearn this unhealthy practice.

Always ask yourself: Do you perceive as glass as something that is half-full or half-empty? True, this question has already been asked, perhaps decades or centuries ago, but the essence and the significance remains. By testing yourself if you are an optimist or a pessimist, then the proper course of actions to overcome fears will be easier to address.

There are related studies wherein it has been established that pessimism and optimism can bring about many effects on a person's health and physical state. But more than that, it has a great effect on a person's point of view. The way they contain fear is greatly affected by this. Positive thinking can help in the effective facilitation of management of stress. Consequently, it can also help in controlling one's fears. On the other hand, pessimists tend to give in to their fears.

Remember, you need to do some positive self-talk to reinforce the value of optimism. By doing positive thinking, one does not necessarily have to ignore the bad things happening around you. Instead, positive thinking teaches individuals to do things in the most productive and positive ways despite the unpleasant solution. You are trained to think that the best can happen despite all the adversities.

Positive thought is often borne out of positive self-talk. Positive self-talk is like a limitless stream of thoughts that are not spoken. They usually run and go on inside your head. For pessimistic people, the stream of thought is usually negative. But for optimists, they choose to keep their self-talk positive at all times.

Remember, if the thoughts are negative, you invite negative situations to occur. You justify the existence of your fears by feeding them so that they will be larger in life.

According to research, aside from successfully beating anxiety, there are many benefits that can be derived from positive self-talk. The following are just some of the examples:

- A significant increase in a person's lifespan
- Lowered rate of depression
- Reduced level of distress
- Higher resistance against flu and colds

- Improved physical and psychological welfare and well-being
- Reduced level of death due to heart attack
- Improved skills in coping up during stress and hardships.

Getting Involved in Physical Activities

Getting physical is one of the most enjoyable ways of fighting your anxiety. By getting more involved in physical activities, you will become more fit and healthy. Your body functions will normalize. The most desirable effect of physical activities is that your levels of anxiety would be reduced. According to the evidence, it can be concluded that anxiety levels can be reduced significantly by doing more exercise.

To be more specific, there are preferred exercise routine that can help reduce fear and anxiety, among these, are:

1. Swimming, running, and biking, among other aerobic exercise routines
2. Long-term programs of exercise (those that take at least twelve to fifteen weeks to complete) rather than those that are short.

Also, it was found out that people who are out of shape derive more benefit from exercise than those who are already fit. Lastly, experiments suggest that those people who have a high level of anxiety levels tend to benefit more from getting involved from physical activities than those who have little or no anxiety.

It was recommended by a series of studies that a person should get involved in at least half an hour of moderate exercise every single day if you want to reap the maximum benefit of getting physical. Increasing the intensity of your exercise routines will not hurt either. There are separate studies attesting to the fact that it can be helpful in making you feel better about yourself.

Examining Your Diet

Foods that Alleviate Anxiety

You can try easing anxiety by eating foods that are rich in nutrients. However, there is no real connection between what types of food work for an individual with anxiety. Still, there is still reason to believe that a well-rounded diet will address the needs of people with anxiety.

Good nutrition and a healthy diet is a must in our daily lives. Deficiencies of omega-3, vitamin D, magnesium, vitamin B complex, folate, amino acids, iron, zinc, iodine, and selenium are highly related to anxiety. But also a high consumption of processed sugar, saturated fat, and trans fats are considered to trigger anxiety. When you eat a lot of these foods, you don't give your body and brain the nutrition needed to function properly. Have balanced and healthy meals and cut all the processed sugars, saturated fats, and trans fats to maximize your mood every day.

Eat Foods with Nutrients

Nutrient-rich foods support the growth, repair, and wellness of one's body. Vitamins, carbohydrates, protein, and minerals are all needed by everyone. Fat in one's diet wouldn't hurt. If you are not able to eat the right amount of nutrients, your body will not function properly and can even make you sick.

Essential Antioxidants on your Plate

Normal body functions cause free radicals which cause dysfunction and aging. Antioxidants fight free radicals. Eat foods high in vitamin C, beta-carotene and vitamin E. The brain is at risk when it comes to free radicals, study shows. These power foods can keep free radicals at bay:

Foods rich in Beta-carotene: broccoli, apricots, carrots, cantaloupe, peaches, collards, spinach, sweet potato, pumpkin

Foods rich in Vitamin C: broccoli, grapefruit, blueberries, oranges, peppers, kiwi. Tomato, strawberries, and potatoes

Foods rich in Vitamin E: seeds and nuts, vegetable oils, wheat germ and margarine

Eat the "Right Carbs" to Calm your Mind

Serotonin, the "feel good mood" correlates carbohydrates. There is a study which says that craving carbohydrates decrease serotonin. With this data in hand, making smart choices when it comes to eating carbs such as avoiding sugary foods, cookies and cakes can be the best choice.

Foods That May Help with Anxiety

Now that we have gone through the food that can worsen anxiety, here is an array of foodstuff which will help it.

Nuts

More specifically almonds, cashews, walnuts and brazil nuts. Eating 1-2 brazil nuts a day is proven to boost an individual's serotonin levels.

Fresh fruit and vegetables

It has always been a known fact that vegetables and fruit are good for you. The benefits have been regularly exclaimed by parents, books and the little pamphlets at the doctor's office. And your mind is not exempt from these benefits; eating fresh produce can work at alleviating a depressed mood. Asparagus, avocado, blueberries, raspberries, and blackberries are especially effective for boosting a mood.

Chamomile and green tea

Chamomile tea should be drunk before you hit the hay as it promotes restful sleep. This means you may have a sleep that is not riddled with anxiety and discomfort. Green tea has a long-winded list of benefits attached to it, including helping with depression. Try to drink 2 cups of green tea a day.

Wholegrain bread

Cottage cheese

Oatmeal

Brain Food

Eat a lot of food that contains omega-3, as this essential fatty acid can work at boosting your mood. Olive oil and most seafood are especially rich in this fatty acid.

Getting Enough Sleep

It begins with how you end your day. Usually, you tend to succumb to fear because your brain and body are not well-rested.

According to research, not having a consistent sleep pattern can entail many serious consequences. So, you should try your best to get as much sleep as you can.

The normal sleep cycle for a better new day is about eight hours long. If you get that much sleep, then it will be more likely for you to wake up with a fresher and better outlook in life.

Lack of sleep is found to be a great contributor to stress, anxiety, and irrational fear. Also, it negatively affects a person's physical health. And it works two ways – lack of sleep lead to anxiety attacks and anxiety attacks lead to sleep disruption.

If you are currently feeling anxious, you should do some serious effort to avoid sleep disruption. You need to allocate eight to ten hours to account for the difficulty in catching some sleep. Also, you need to free yourself from the thoughts that are giving you stress.

Relax your Breathing

Not everyone is given the privilege to breathe freely and easily. You need to enjoy this privilege to the fullest, and you will be surprised because it can help you fight your fears and anxiety.

Try to practice your deep breathing exercises regularly. You have to find a spot where you won't just be disturbed by anyone. As much as possible, that place should be quiet – quiet enough so that you can hear your own breathing. In the process, you might need to loosen up your clothing and remove the tight ones. This will help you feel as comfortable as possible.

Find your most comfortable chair. Make sure that you will support your head properly. Or you can choose to lie down on a bed or the floor. Put your hands on the side with your palms facing up. If you choose to lie down, try to stretch your legs out in such a way that you keep them apart. If you are sitting on a chair, by all means, do not cross your legs because it might hamper free breathing.

For better breathing, you need to relax. Try to do this as slowly as possible and find your regular and natural rhythm. These steps will help you calm down."

1. Fill your lungs with all the air that you can take in. Be careful not to force air in. Try to fill your lungs from the bottom.

2. When taking in air, use your nose. When breathing out, use your mouth.

3. Try to breathe in as slowly as possible. To make it regular, try to count from one to five while completing the breathing cycle. In the beginning, you will notice that it is difficult to reach five.

4. Do the same for breathing out.

5. Try to do this repeatedly until you calm your nerves. Continue breathing without any pause. As much as possible, do not hold your breath back.

Relaxed breathing should be done from 3 to 5 minutes, at least three times a day. If you are stressed or anxious, doing this more often might help.

Meditation

At this point, there is a need to define what meditation truly is. Yes, you may have an idea that it is a well-known relaxation method, but science tells us that it is much more than that. Through a series of research, it was found out that meditation leads to the increase in the brain's grey matter. In simplified terms, meditation finds a way to rewire the body so that it will feel less stress for putting the same amount of effort. In the end, it shields you from feeling fear and anxiety.

In much more recent research efforts, it was suggested that meditation has a good effect on brain activity. It can control mood, stress, and anxiety. Since it is relaxing, meditation can help in blocking thoughts that can provoke your fears and anxiety.

However, there is a proper way of doing meditation. If you do it right, you will find rest, and you will even feel energized and renewed. Proper meditation can bring about the rest, and it can dissolve your anxiety and stress. Your body has the innate capability to take care of stress while you sleep. However, if you are not able to get enough rest, stress and insomnia might ensue.

If you wish to combat stress and anxiety, you might want to choose TM or transcendental meditation.

This is a technique that is proven scientifically to provide the body one of the deepest known state of rest. It can bring about coherence to your brain waves. Within a cycle of twenty minutes' worth of meditation, you will find yourself more alert. Also, fatigue and stress would be instantly reduced. According to research, transcendental meditation can give you peacefulness and calmness.

Relax your Muscles

Believe it or not, this technique will only take twenty minutes of your time. All you need to do is stretch some of your muscle groups and bring them down to their relaxed state. This way, you will successfully release all the tension that you are hiding inside your body. The relaxation of the body and the relaxation of your mind will soon follow.

Here's what you should do: First, you need to find your favorite spot – preferably one that is quiet and warm. That place should have no distractions. Then, you can sit or lie down there. You need to close your eyes and start to focus on your breathing – trying to do it as slowly and as deeply as you can.

Identify your aching muscles. Focus on those muscles longer and spend time relaxing them.

Then, to help you in relaxing further, you might want to play your favorite music. It should be the soothing kind of music, not the distracting type. Note that there are different groups of muscles that you need to focus on:

1. Facial muscles – there is a need to push the eyebrows in such a way that they will meet each

other. The resulting facial expression is similar to that of frowning. After that, you may release.

2. Neck muscles – Tilt your head gently forwards. Then, push your chin downwards towards the chest and lift it slowly again.

3. Shoulder muscles – Pull each of your shoulders towards the corresponding ear and then try to relax them as you move each along the direction of the corresponding foot.

4. Chest muscles – Try to breathe as slowly as possible and make sure that you are feeling your diaphragm. This is located just below the bottom rib. This way, you can be sure that you are utilizing your entire lungs. Try to breath out slowly and allow your belly to deflate until all the air inside your lungs is released.

5. Arm muscles – Try to stretch each of your arms away from your body. Reach for the farthest point you can for a few seconds, and then relax.

6. Leg muscles – Push each of your toes away from your body and then pull each of them towards your body. Now, try to relax.

7. Wrist muscles – try to stretch each of your wrists by trying to pull each of your hand up towards your direction. Then, gently pull each of your fingers. After this, you are ready to relax your wrist.

Do the entire routine using as much time as you need. More importantly, try doing these while your eyes are closed so that you can find peace with yourself.

Practicing Mindfulness

Mindfulness is an effective tool to stop rumination and worrying. This involves a process of putting into use the non-judgmental type of awareness to present or express one's emotions and thoughts. It serves as a strategy in the cognitive and behavioral therapy.

According to studies, mindfulness can help in beating fear and anxiety because it encourages people to change their style of thinking. Also, they are expected to disengage from worry and rumination as a method of emotional response. With mindfulness, people tend to dwell on thinking of more specific and more concrete methods of finding solutions. Experts call this phenomenon as the cognitive to restructure thinking. This encourages a more positive approach to thinking.

Mindfulness, however, should not be misunderstood as a method of coming up with direct solutions to complicated problems. Be warned, however, that things are not that simple. Instead, mindfulness should be thought of as a technique or skill. It is a strategy to control your attention, and this can be improved by training daily and continuously.

By doing systematic training of mindfulness, you can significantly improve the manner by which you handle your anxiety. Even patients of depression are helped out by mindfulness techniques.

Turn Fears into Inspirations

To beat your fears, you need to find a way to transform them into inspiration. To help you out, there are at least four methods to transform your fears into sources of inspiration successfully.

1. Live in the simplest manner possible. If you are not familiar with the minimalist type of lifestyle, you can start researching about that now. In essence, it will help you to go back to basics. It will teach you not to hold on to material stuff. By leading a simple kind of life, you will have less reason to fear.

2. Write down everything. Often, when your mind is filled with ideas – be it bright or dull – you are too afraid that you might lose them all. Never trust your rusty memory! Write everything down so that you can free up your brain. You can keep a notepad and a pen in your car, in your bedroom, and in the office. Or you can use your mobile device to do this successfully.

3. Chill! A body filled with anxiety is a body that lacks relaxation. There are techniques that you can subscribe to to improve your sleep and relaxation regimen. The best news is that most of them are free.

4. Change the mental habits that keep you stuck to your fears and anxiety. The way you think can improve the way you view your life.

To transform your fears into inspiration, you need to be at ease with yourself. However, many people say that they are too busy to be at ease. This is a problem because one has to truly willing before positive results can be obtained. But you can never too busy

If you truly want to turn your life around. If your life is bound to change for the better, then you have to do whatever it takes. And yes, most of the time, techniques usually take only a few minutes to change the way you think. And the techniques are not complicated at all.

Have an open mind. And changing anxiety or fears into inspiration involves many steps, but it begins with having an open mind. This will help you find your way out of anxiety and living an inspired life.

You have to consciously guide your mind to move away from unskillful and counter-productive emotions like fear, anger, and anxiety. You need to find a way to replace these with cheerfulness and kindness – these are the key to real happiness.

Chapter 5: Action Plan I – Dealing with Anxious Thoughts

Nothing impacts your thoughts as much as anxiety. Suddenly, the world comes to a standstill, and you begin to think that everyday things and situations may be threatening to you. The feeling that everything is going wrong and you will not be able to deal with the situation makes anxiety psychologically dangerous.

You may start finding normal situations, or situations that seemed normal to you the last time they occurred, potentially dangerous. For instance, having a cough may bother you and force you to think that you are suffering from some chronic disorder of which coughing is a symptom, or your child is 10 minutes from school may compel to think about all the wrong things that could have happened to him.

As a general rule, people with anxiety live under the constant fear that something is going wrong so much so that they may be dreadful to cope with. What they fear is not just the situation, but also the fact that they won't be able to manage them and remain calm and safe in it. This is a vicious circle of sorts. When you feel anxious, you are surrounded by thoughts of fear, thread, and avoidance. Moreover, when you consider a situation negative or threatening, you are likely to get anxious about it.

What you think directly impacts what you feel, and if you can curb your thoughts, your anxiety levels will automatically drop. Let us take the example of two ladies who are waiting for their children to come home from a party, late at night. Their children are out of a party and had promised to come back by 11 that night. The first lady begins to panic as the clock strikes 11, and every minute past that time her anxiety levels rise. To add to her misery, she begins to think about all the bad things that could have happened to her child, which adds up to the anxiety substantially.

The second lady also gets anxious to find out why her child is not back at 11. However, she remembers all the times when her child had promised to be back by a certain time and had arrived 10 minutes late, so her anxiety levels drop. In both the cases, the ladies got anxious, however, while the first lady increased her anxiety levels by thinking about things that escalated her worrying, the second lady thought of things that helped her manage her anxiety.

Suffice to say; thoughts have a significant impact on your overall anxiety levels. An increased anxiety level will translate into more serious physical symptoms. The best way to manage the scenario is to break the cycle of anxiety and thoughts by thinking from a positive and constructive perspective.

To help you manage anxious thoughts, you need to give yourself some time and follow the two-step exercise explained below.

1. The first step is to identify the thoughts that are making you anxious.
2. The second step is to replace these thoughts with alternative thoughts which are more constructive and realistic.

As we move forward in this chapter, we shall explore these two steps in greater detail and how you can implement them in your daily life.

You cannot challenge anxiety unless you know the cause behind it. This is exactly the reason why identifying anxious thoughts is extremely important. With this said, it is equally important to state that this identification process will not be simple. Such thoughts are automatic and so quick in occurring that you don't even realize that something you thought just raised your anxiety levels. Fortunately, the effects of anxiety are such that you will know that you are anxious and applying reverse psychology to the cause is the only option that lies with you. As you practice, identifying such thoughts will get easier.

Typically, anxious thoughts that take the shape of "what if" and "I don't think I can cope." If you have experienced an embarrassing situation lately or an incident that has had a grave impact on your mind, then reliving the incident in our mind may also be a cause of anxiety. The most challenging aspect of identifying anxious thoughts is that you are already anxious, and being able to control your mind at such time for an analysis of this degree may be tough.

Therefore, it is a good idea to have well-framed questions to ask yourself every single time you get anxious. For instance, as yourself:

- Why am I feeling this way?
- How did it start?
- Are all my assumptions actually true?
- Will this actually happen?
- How will this impact me, my life, and the people around me?

How to Start?

Prepare a Thought Record

As you perform this activity, be sure to record your thoughts and answers in a diary. This will help you analyze the situation with a calmer mind at a later time. In this way, you will be able to use the information gathered for managing anxiety for future instances even if you weren't able to help yourself at the time it occurred. This record sheet can also play an instrumental role in determining behavioral patterns and identifying underlying issues if any are present.

Determine the Realistic Thoughts from Anxious Thoughts

Once the identification process is complete, and you know how to do it at the time of anxiety, as well as analyze the pattern over a period, the next step is to determine if the thoughts are realistic. Most anxious thoughts are actually assumptions or exaggerated reactions to situations. Therefore, this step will help you get a realistic and objective viewpoint on the situation.

Moving forward, you must look for an alternative way of thinking about the situation. This is a daunting task, and you will need to practice this method a lot before you can be an expert on it. In the previous step, you had prepared a thoughts record. In this step, you may add two columns to the thought record, one each for evidence that supports your thought and the one that goes against it. Use these columns to create a new column, which gives an alternative and realistic thought for replacing the existing anxious thought.

Assessment

No method is effective unless it can help you reduce your anxiety levels. Therefore, before you sit down to write the record: assess your anxiety levels by rating it on a scale from 1 to 10; 1 being the least anxious and ten being the highest. Rate your anxiety levels after you have evaluated the alternative thought using the method illustrated here. This will help you know if the method is working for you.

Chapter 6: Action Plan II – Dealing with Worries

Understanding Worrying

People who complain of anxiety usually worry a lot; much more than they should. If you are a chronic worrier, the chances are that you worry about a lot of things. Therefore, you will have some worry topics in your mind. As you learn to manage one worry topic, your mind may switch to another one. It soon becomes evident that it is not the incidents that are the problem; the problem lies within you, and in the manner you perceive things. Therefore, what you need to manage is not the situation, but you need to manage your self.

Another thing that you need to understand is that worrying is a maze on its own. If you believe that worrying is a bad thing, then you will worry about the very fact that you worry. On the other hand, if you start believing that worrying is good, you will continue to worry about that isn't worrying enough.

Touching on the negative effects of worrying, some people worry about worrying and how it can negatively affect them. Such thoughts usually take the shape of worrying about the fact that worrying has gone out of control or realizing that it is harmful and not being able to do anything about it.

What is even worse is that you don't even know if you are worrying too much about worrying. To determine this, you must question yourself about whether worrying is a problem, and what is the worst that can happen to you if you continue to worry. Lastly, a quick assessment on whether it is possible for you to stop worrying can bring about decent closure to the situation.

While talking about concerns and worries, the one thing about worrying that is most disturbing for people is the fact that they are not able to control their feelings. To challenge this belief, the first thing that you must do is to look for an incident where you were worried. Assess the situation to answer a few questions:

- Was it possible for you to control your worries?
- How hard did you stop worrying?
- Were you able to stop these worries in the end?
- If yes, what was the cause of this stoppage?

Now that you have analyzed the situation in full look at your anxiety situation in its entirety.

- How often have you worried, and were you able to control your worries?
- Can you think of any incident when you were able to get rid of your worries successfully? If yes, how?

By the end of this analysis, you will be in a better position to assess whether your worrying situation is controllable or not. The biggest problem with controlling worries and anxious thoughts is that it is rather difficult to control or suppress them. When you try to get rid of such thoughts and think of something else, you are likely to come back to these anxiety-provoking thoughts no matter what. It is a human psychology to think more of the things that you think of not thinking. For example, if I ask you to not think about the white pigeon, images of it will keep coming back to your mind all the time.

How Can You Manage Worrying?

Controlled worry periods is a concept that shall help you in this endeavor. When you can accomplish this a couple of times, you will get a sense of control over the situation, which shall be instrumental in helping you break the vicious cycle of uncontrollable worrying.

The concept of controlled worry period is based on the fact that you must set out a fixed length of time, place, and exact time for worrying. This should be the same time every single day.

Whenever you feel like worrying, you must tell yourself that you will take up this issue at a later time that is set aside for worrying. While you can choose any time of the day for this activity, it is best to avoid performing this right before bedtime.

1. Spend no more than 15 minutes worrying about all the things you had marked during the day.
2. Brainstorm by yourself, and the moment you decide that the matter is not worth worrying about anymore, you must stop worrying about it.

To ensure that you don't forget any of the agendas that you had set for the worrying period, jot down your worries for the day on a notepad set aside for this purpose. The beauty of this method is that it plays with your psychology in such a way that you are not asking your mind to stop worrying. You are actually giving it a later appointment for worrying.

Chapter 7: Action Plan III – Dealing with Avoidance

When a situation makes you feel anxious, it is understandable and obvious that you will try to avoid the situation at any cost. This is, in actuality, a short-term solution to your problem. You will avoid the situation, and you will not have to face it. Therefore, for the moment, it is a good strategy to get rid of anxiety. However, when you talk about the long-term impact of anxiety, you will realize that such a behavior lessens your chances of being able to cope with anxiety in the future.

Let us take the example of an individual who fears social situations and avoids attending social gatherings. Her friends ask her out for coffee, but she makes an excuse. In other words, she avoids the situation. However, when her same friends ask her out again, she is likely to feel all the more anxious about meeting her friends because she had not met them from the last time, and she will have to explain declining another invitation.

In a way, the girl was anxious about being a part of a social gathering, so she avoided the situation. While this avoidance helped her manage the situation at that time, it did not make any substantial contribution in helping her face such situations that may encounter in the future, and the next time she is faced with such a situation she will feel anxious again. You need to break this cycle to manage your anxiety problem.

Obviously, not facing the issue will not help you in any way. You will have to face the situation and break the cycle. Feeling anxious is natural and fine, in some cases. You don't have to believe that there is something abnormal about the fact that you are feeling anxious.

Moreover, once you face the situation, you will realize the anxiety levels have automatically gone down. This will also reduce the anxiety levels that you will experience the next time you face a similar situation.

Three Things You Can Do Towards Managing Avoidance

First, ever assume that you will be able to get rid of all your anxiety the first time you encounter an anxiety-provoking situation. It is a gradual process.

Secondly, in your attempts to manage anxiety, you must face an anxiety-provoking situation that is least anxiety-provoking.

Once you can face it, you will rise in confidence and will be in a much better position to face a greater anxiety-provoking situation that the last one. Lastly, it is a good idea to make a list of all the things that make you anxious. Although this activity will be anxiety-provoking and a lot of hard work for you, it can be a great way to deal with the situations when they face you.

Final Words

Anxiety is something that is prevalent in our modern society. It has already reached a point wherein everyone is a potential victim, and they might not even know about it. It truly is a negative experience, and the levels of intensity may vary. If you are struggling with fear and anxiety, you might feel that you are hopeless. It might even feel like it would be impossible for you to overcome it. But here's the good news: there are physical and mental options to reduce the anxiety levels. There are discussed fully in this book.

I hope that this book has helped you point out anxiety right at its course. If you recently struggled with fear and anxiety attack, you need to fight it right away by identifying the root of the problem. On a recap, this book has guided you to answer the following questions:

a. Can you identify the source of anxiety in your immediate environment?

b. Is there an unfortunate event that can be a possible source of your anxiety?

c. Is there a meeting, event, or activity that might trigger your anxiety?

After due identification of the source of fear, you can easily apply ways and action plans presented in this book.

From the answers you obtain, you can easily tell if your fears and worries are solvable. By knowing your anxiety, you can tell if you have enough faculties to deal with it accordingly.

Remember, there are instances wherein only time can solve the problem, and you can't do anything about it. If you think that the source of your anxiety is brought about your imagination, you need to make some serious effort to take it off your consciousness. If you think that the source of fear is something real, then you need to follow the given action plan and answer the following questions:

a. What can be done to reduce the intensity of your anxiety?

b. Can it be fixed within a short period or will you need some time?

c. To stop the problem from recurring, what can be done?

Conclusion

I hope this book was able to help you manage your anxiety issues. No matter how you choose to manage your anxiety, remember that there is nothing abnormal about being anxious. Try to remember that the things you are experiencing anxiety over are things that don't deserve such reaction from you.

There is no quick fix or a solution that fits all when it comes to managing anxiety. It will require a lot of hard work from your end. You will need to practice the techniques described in this book and use when required in your best capacity to get the most out of them.

The next step is to go ahead and use the information in this book.

About the Co-Author

My name is George Kaplo; I'm a certified personal trainer from Montreal, Canada. I'll start off by saying I'm not the biggest guy you will ever meet and this has never really been my goal. In fact, I started working out to overcome my biggest insecurity when I was younger, which was my self-confidence. This was due to my height measuring only 5 foot 5 inches (168cm), it pushed me down to attempt anything I ever wanted to achieve in life. You may be going through some challenges right now, or you may simply want to get fit, and I can certainly relate.

For me personally, I was always kind of interested in the health & fitness world and wanted to gain some muscle due to the numerous bullying in my teenage years about my height and my overweight body. I figured I couldn't do anything about my height, but I sure can do something about how my body looked like. This was the beginning of my transformation journey. I had no idea where to start, but I just got started. I felt worried and afraid at times that other people would make fun of me for doing the exercises the wrong way. I always wished I had a friend that was next to me who was knowledgeable enough to help me get started and "show me the ropes."

After a lot of work, studying and countless trial and errors. Some people began to notice how I was getting more fit and how I was starting to form a keen interest in the topic. This led many friends and new faces to come to me and ask me for fitness advice. At first, it seemed odd when people asked me to help them get in shape. But what kept me going is when they started to see changes in their own body and told me it's the first time that they saw real results! From there, more people kept coming to me, and it made me realize after so much reading and studying in this field that it did help me but it also allowed me to help others. I'm now a fully certified personal trainer and have trained numerous clients to date who have achieved amazing results.

Today, my brother Alex Kaplo (also a Certified Personal Trainer) and I own & operate this publishing venture, where we bring passionate and expert authors to write about health and fitness topics. We also run an online fitness website "HelpMeWorkout.com" and I would love to connect with by inviting you to visit the website on the following page and signing up to our e-mail newsletter (you will even get a free book).

Last but not least, if you are in the position I was once in and you want some guidance, don't hesitate and ask... I'll be there to help you out!

Your friend and coach

George Kaplo

Certified Personal Trainer

Download another book for Free

I want to thank you for purchasing this book and offer you another book (just as long and valuable as this book), "Health & Fitness Mistakes You Don't Know You're Making", completely free.

Visit the link below to signup and receive it: www.hmwpublishing.com/gift

In this book, I will break down the most common health & fitness mistakes, you are probably committing right now, and I will reveal how you can easily get in the best shape of your life!

In addition to this valuable gift, you will also have an opportunity to get our new books for free, enter giveaways, and receive other valuable emails from me. Again, visit the link to sign up: www.hmwpublishing.com/gift

Copyright 2017 by HMW Publishing - All Rights Reserved.

This document by HMW Publishing owned by the A&G Direct Inc company, is geared towards providing exact and reliable information in regards to the topic and issue covered. The publication is sold with the idea that the publisher is not required to render accounting, officially permitted, or otherwise, qualified services. If advice is necessary, legal or professional, a practiced individual in the profession should be ordered.

From a Declaration of Principles which was accepted and approved equally by a Committee of the American Bar Association and a Committee of Publishers and Associations.

In no way is it legal to reproduce, duplicate, or transmit any part of this document in either electronic means or in printed format. Recording of this publication is strictly prohibited, and any storage of this document is not allowed unless with written permission from the publisher. All rights reserved.

The information provided herein is stated to be truthful and consistent, in that any liability, in terms of inattention or otherwise, by any usage or abuse of any policies, processes, or directions contained within is the solitary and utter responsibility of the recipient reader. Under no circumstances will any legal responsibility or blame be held against the publisher for any reparation, damages, or monetary loss due to the information herein, either directly or indirectly.

The information herein is offered for informational purposes solely, and is universal as so. The presentation of the information is without contract or any type of guarantee assurance.

The trademarks that are used are without any consent, and the publication of the trademark is without permission or backing by the trademark owner. All trademarks and brands within this book are for clarifying purposes only and are the owned by the owners themselves, not affiliated with this document.

For more great books visit:

HMWPublishing.com

www.ingramcontent.com/pod-product-compliance
Lightning Source LLC
Chambersburg PA
CBHW070922080526
44589CB00013B/1403